David Attenborough's
FABULOUS ANIMAL

For centuries, people have been fascinated by strange animals. Travellers' tales of creatures they had glimpsed were enlarged and embroidered until it was regarded as fact that giants, dragons, sea-serpents, mermaids and unicorns really did inhabit the unknown parts of the earth.

David Attenborough, whose searches for rare animals have taken him to many distant lands, looks at some of these stories and legends. Is there a Loch Ness Monster? Does the yeti live in the Himalayan mountains? Do other giant creatures remain to be discovered?

Fabulous Animals is fully illustrated, and many of the pictures come from early books of natural history. It is based on the BBC TV children's programme series.

David Attenborough's

FABULOUS ANIMALS

MOLLY COX

AND

DAVID ATTENBOROUGH

Containing

HERE BE MONSTERS

MERMAIDS
and other Marvels of the Sea

DRAGONS AND SERPENTS

WINGED CREATURES

HORNS OF MAGIC

MAN OR BEAST

British Broadcasting Corporation

Published by the
British Broadcasting Corporation,
35 Marylebone High Street,
London W1M 4AA

ISBN 0 563 17006 9

First published 1975

Printed in England by
Lowe and Brydone (Printers) Ltd,
Thetford, Norfolk

Acknowledgement is due to the following
for permission to reproduce illustrations:
Lutterworth Press, page 49 (from *Zoo
Quest to Madagascar*); Bruce Coleman Ltd.,
page 43; British Museum, page 11;
Mansell Collection, page 50.

HERE BE MONSTERS

ND METHUSELAH lived nine hundred and sixty-nine years before he died ... and Noah was five hundred years old ... There were giants in the earth in those days ... the mighty men of old.

Stories of giants and curious monsters go back to ancient times – they come from the Bible, from Anglo-Saxon legends, and from ancient Greece and Rome.

Why have people always been so fascinated by these wondrous tales of huge creatures? It has been said "Science begins with wondering ... " and it must have been very wonderful indeed – quite awe-inspiring – the first time an explorer came face to face with a wild animal he had never seen before. When he told the story afterwards, he probably made it worth telling.

I have spent a fair amount of time searching for rare animals in remote parts of the world, and have been lucky enough to find and film some of them too. And among the things that have spurred me on – as with other travellers – are the old books with stories and pictures about animals handed down from previous centuries.

"The Crocodile is a devouring and insatiable beast. The body is rough, being covered all over with a certain bark or rinde; so thick, firm and strong as it is impenetrable with any dart or spear, yea scarcely to a pistol or small gun; but the belly is softer. This monstrous serpent groweth all his life long unto the length of fifteen or twenty cubits."

That description comes from a book published in 1658. Fifteen or twenty cubits would be about twenty-five to thirty feet. It is hard to remember accurately what you have seen without cameras to record it. In 1658 it could take a year or more to make your way home from Africa or India.

In 1599 a European traveller who saw a giraffe in the Sultan's menagerie in Constantinople wrote: "It is a strange and wonderful beast, the like of which has never been seen before. It has a long neck like a camel and is spotted like a panther."

The animal was thought then to be a hybrid, a mixture of the two animals, and so it was called a camelopard. The word giraffe comes from the Arabic word *zirafa*, which means "the lovely one". The Saracens admired this animal with its huge eyes and long lashes so much that they wrote poems about its beauty.

The first sight of a strange animal used to make people exaggerate their strangeness. When the animals are big as well they can become monsters in stories, and the really large animals that we know – the whale and the African elephant – are so huge they are still worth wondering at.

Whales are probably the largest animals that have ever lived. The blue whale can grow to be one hundred and thirty feet long and weigh one hundred and seventy tons. At full speed it can travel up to twenty knots – that needs a force of five hundred horsepower. In ancient days it was thought that a whale would deliberately pretend to be an island, and lie still in the water until sailors landed on it. Then it would dive deep into the water and drown them. Sadly, in the last century, man has hunted the large whales almost to extinction.

Elephants have gathered about themselves a long list of legends too. One is that they never forget. Some recent experiments show that although it may take a long time to teach elephants, once having learned something they will remember with amazing accuracy even a year later. It was once believed that elephants ate flowers because they liked the sweet smell. And many people believe that when Hannibal took his fighting elephants from Carthage across the Alps and down into Italy, it was just the sight of them that caused the

A drawing of an elephant from a sixteenth-century book of natural history

Roman armies to fail. But in fact, out of the fifty war elephants he brought from Africa, only eight reached the battlefield and only one survived to go home to Carthage. It has also been said that elephants are afraid of mice – but that story isn't true.

For years stories have been told about old elephants leaving the herd and taking themselves off to a secret part of the forest to die, in a mysterious graveyard. In the nineteenth century – and even in this – the ivory hunters of Africa were always hoping to discover this hidden elephants' graveyard and make their fortunes from selling the valuable hoard of tusks. The origin of the legend goes back nearly 2,000 years. It was first told by the Romans:

"At the foot of these mountains where the forests are deepest with dense and shady groves ... elephants are said to resort in old age ... Nature leads them there to a colony, giving them rest at last ... where they can live out the last years of their life ... They have an agreement with the barbarians of those parts that they shall not be hunted."

But that is a colony that no one has yet found.

Even stranger than the stories about giant animals are all the legends about giant men. From fairy tales come Jack the giant killer, Jack and the beanstalk, and Finn McCool. Finn McCool is said to have built the Giants' Causeway in Ireland, and the English giant stories are very old indeed. Centuries ago, huge figures of giants were carved into the chalk on the side of hills; in Sussex the Long Man of Wilmington, in Dorset the giant of Cerne Abbas. Gog and Magog are twin giants whose statues stood for hundreds of years in London's Guildhall, and used to be carried in procession round the boundaries of the City. In parts of Scotland and Ireland there are legends that giants are turned to stone if they are caught by the sunrise when out walking at night. Red Indians have the same sort of stories of men turned to stone by magic. In Wales there are old stories of caves where gigantic men – the Ancient Kings – lie sleeping, waiting for some call that will break the spell and awaken them.

What could have caused all these giant stories? In lonely parts of Scotland you can still be told of road-diggers coming across the grave of some legendary hero – "the giant of a man twelve feet high!" Only a fairy story? Well partly; but what would you think if you were digging the foundations of a road through some wild lonely mountains and came across a thigh bone five feet long. You might well consider it proof that once there really were giants in Britain!

For hundreds of years, all over Europe huge "stone-bones" were found. There were many guesses about what they were, the bones of dragons, the bones of giants, and so on. In 1676 a British naturalist called Robert Plot put some of them together. He shaped them into the skeleton of a man seventeen feet high and exhibited his giant in Switzerland for everyone to wonder at. Then, slowly, people began to realise that the bones were not human at all. They were the bones of unknown animals, turned to stone – fossilised and preserved by natural accidents through many millions of years.

Some of these new-found monsters proved to be huge reptiles which had disappeared from the earth over sixty million years ago. A word was invented to describe them, a word meaning "terrible lizards" – dinosaurs.

In 1877 deep down in a coal mine in Belgium, colliers were digging out a new tunnel. Suddenly they were aware of a strange smell – a smell of swamps – and found they were digging out something that looked like the ribs of a giant ox – a monster skeleton. They found more and more of these strange black and heavy bones.

There were huge thigh bones, shoulders and skulls, and very carefully they brought them in buckets to the surface. It took years to piece them all together, and then it was discovered they had found no less than thirty complete dinosaurs. Lying between the coal seams for millions of years had been these perfect skeletons of thirty Iguanadons. Now these are the pride of the Royal Belgian Natural History Museum.

A replica of one of the Belgian Iguanadons is in the Natural History Museum in London where there are skeletons of many other dinosaurs. The biggest of them is the Diplodocus. It lived about a hundred million years or so before the first men appeared on earth. Although it was eighty-four feet long, it was probably fairly harmless. It was a plant-eater, and spent most of its time in swamps champing through the vegetation with the water helping to support its immense body.

The Tyrannosaurus rex, though, was very different. It had teeth six inches long in its massive jaws, and was undoubtedly a flesh eater. It walked upright on its massive hind legs, its front legs were just tiny stumps, and it weighed seven tons. It was probably the most ferocious beast that ever walked the face of the earth.

Fossilised tracks of such giant creatures have been found, some in Dorset, and you can see these in the museum. These footprints give us very valuable evidence about how the various dinosaurs looked when they were alive, how they moved and how much muscle and flesh they had on their feet. From the shape of their teeth, their jaws and the formation of their bones we can discover much more. But just occasionally fossils have been found with the impression of their actual skin preserved, and from this we know that some dinosaurs had knobbly bony plates on their backs. And so we can put together with some degree of accuracy the whole fantastic appearance of these magnificent creatures

A reconstruction of Tyrannosaurus rex

which lived on the earth long before any man.

It is odd to think that it is only in the last two hundred years that all those creatures – the Brontosaurus, the Pterodactyls, the Plesiosaurus, and Tyrannosaurus rex have been discovered after they had been dead and totally lost to sight for millions and millions of years. Now dinosaurs are so accepted that they even get made into plastic toys to be given away with breakfast cereals! But imagine how exciting it was when people were first piecing together these huge vanished monsters.

My favourite dinosaur discovery story is one about an American expedition which went to the lonely Gobi Desert in Mongolia – to a desolate place they called Flaming Cliffs. This is how one of them described it: "Our arrival at Flaming Cliffs was a great day for the Central Asiatic Expedition. We camped at three o'clock in the afternoon and almost at once the men scattered over the badlands. Before night everyone had discovered a dinosaur skull.

"But the real thrill came the second day when George Olsen reported that he was sure he had found some fossil eggs. We joked with him a good deal but, nevertheless, were curious enough to go down with him after luncheon. Then our indifference suddenly evaporated. It was certain they really were eggs. Three of them were exposed and had evidently broken out of the sandstone ledge beside which they lay. Other shell fragments were partially embedded in the rock and just under the shelf we could see the ends of two more eggs.

"While the rest of us were on our hands and knees about the spot, Olsen scraped away the loose rock on the summit of the ledge. To our amazement he uncovered the skeleton of a small dinosaur lying four inches above the eggs. Almost certainly these were the first dinosaur eggs ever seen by modern human eyes.

"In shape the specimens were elongated, much like a loaf of French bread, and were totally unlike the eggs of any known birds, turtles, or reptiles. Two of them, broken in half, showed the white bones of unhatched baby dinosaurs. The preservation was beautiful. Some of the eggs had been crushed, but the pebbled surface of the shells was as perfect as though they had been laid yesterday instead of eighty or ninety million years ago."

Though the accidental finding of dinosaur eggs and bones through the ages might explain some of the legends and fables about giants, there were other monsters that once lived – not millions of years ago like the dinosaurs but at the same time as early man.

Our ancestors hunted the sabre-toothed tiger, the woolly rhinoceros and the long-haired mammoth, and drew pictures of them on the walls of their caves. Some of the "giant-bones" found in caves turned out to be the preserved bones of these extinct creatures. Mammoths had become extinct, but stories about them still persisted. In Russia and in Lapland, people used to tell stories about mysterious monsters which burrowed deep down under the ice and snow and lived alone in dark underground passages. It was said that if they accidentally dug their way up to the surface, they died as soon as they reached daylight, and this was proved by the curved ivory tusks which were often found sticking up out of the frozen ground. It is true that valuable ivory was brought to the west. In fact, for hundreds of years there was a flourishing trade in mammoth tusks. Other stories were told of men who had actually come face to face with a whole huge hairy mammoth, locked in a block of ice; and fled in terror – only to discover when at last they came creeping back that the terrible thing had melted away and vanished!

Then, early in this century, in 1901, a Russian scientific expedition set off on a long journey. A Cossack trader had just found a well-preserved mammoth head protruding from the icy ground in Siberia. The expedition took all summer to cross the muddy swamps of the Siberian tundra, and by the time they reached the spot winter had already started. To their delight the mammoth was still there, and it was not just a head, but a complete deep-frozen creature. It lay in the exact position, by the edge of a small cliff, where it originally fell to its death thousands of years earlier. The frozen swamp had completely preserved the animal, and now a small landslide had revealed it. Its flesh was in such perfect condition that wolves had already eaten a little of it, and the camp dogs were only too ready to take a few more bites. A tent was put up to stop the remains from becoming frozen again, and keep the wolves out; and then the investigation began.

Doing a post-mortem on a twenty-five-thousand-year-old monster in a tent in the icy Siberian winter could not have been easy, but it was very exciting as it was the first complete body of a mammoth to be

Mammoth, from a nineteenth-century drawing

properly examined. They discovered that the creature was not much bigger than an ordinary elephant, but its shaggy hair was more than a foot long and rusty-black. Some of its bones had been broken by its original fatal fall down the cliff. In its mouth there were still traces of food, and the contents of its stomach showed that its last meal had been of meadow-grasses and wild flowers. From the state of these flowers they could even tell that it was autumn when the animal fell down the cliff.

The valuable mammoth remains were carefully brought back to Leningrad and reconstructed, and are still shown in the Museum there. Unfortunately the wolves had eaten rather too much of the animal's behind before the scientists could stop them, so it had to be modelled in a somewhat strange position as if sitting down. Other mammoths have been found since, but this 1901 Russian mammoth is still the best to be seen anywhere. Bones of mammoths have been found all over Europe and in this country too, so how was it that all these beautiful beasts died out? Did our ancestors hunt them all to extinction, just as we are doing with the blue whale? Or was there perhaps some sudden change of climate which wiped out their food supplies – so they starved to death? Such a large vegetarian animal would have needed huge quantities of food. The theory usually accepted is that the mammoth herds followed the melting glaciers at the end of the last ice age. They travelled north-east across Europe until they came to the frozen Siberian marshes. There, the layer of frozen top-soil was too thin to bear their great weight. The mammoths fell through to the icy mud below, were trapped and died. Their frozen bodies have been preserved beneath the permafrost ever since. And from time to time a shift in the earth would reveal a carcass. So, the old legends had *some* truth in them.

Some modern zoologists even think that not all the

mammoths may have followed each other blindly to death, and that somewhere in the vast, half-explored forests of Siberia some may still exist. There are three million square miles of forest so it would be possible for some animals to live there unseen. Tantalisingly, there are continual rumours of peasants having glimpsed mysterious beasts with large tusks and chestnut-coloured hair wandering through the larch and pine trees. Could these be mammoths? Who knows – legends and rumours have been right before.

There is another extinct monster with a similar history. The fossilised bones of the giant ground sloth were first found in different parts of South America. Quite a lot was known about it. Standing on its hind legs it was about fifteen feet high. It was heavy and could not run fast. Its teeth proved it lived on vegetable matter, leaves and grasses, and its large claws showed that it could pull up roots. Its skin was hairy and embedded in it were tiny bony nodules. The native Indians had two legends about it. One, like the mammoth, said it was an underground animal, a giant mole which burrowed its way to the surface to die in the daylight. The other story told of a monster, very much alive, a wolf as big as a bull which slept in a cave during the day and roamed about at night. It had thick hairy legs, with huge claws, and lived near water. No arrows could hurt it because it had skin like armour. The first Spanish explorers of South America wrote descriptions of large nocturnal animals which have never been seen since.

"There is a Region in the New-found World, called Gigantes, and the inhabitants thereof are called Patagones; now because their country is cold, being far in the South, they clothe themselves with the skins of a Beast called in their own tongue Su, which signifies water. When the Hunters that desire her skin set upon

A sixteenth-century drawing of a "Su" from the description given by the Spanish explorers

her, she flyeth very swift, carrying her young ones upon her back. There was never any of them taken alive. No arrow can pierce her skin, so they dig a pit and catch her in that way. They take the skin and leave her carcass in the earth."

These legends weren't taken seriously until something very strange happened. A Swedish explorer was travelling through Southern Patagonia and arrived at the outside gates of a ranch. The name of the ranch above the gate was "Ultima Esperanza" (*The Last Hope*). Suddenly something strange caught his eye. Draped across the gateway was a large piece of wild-animal skin, of a type he'd never seen before. The hair was coarse and long, and beneath the hair the skin was covered all over with tiny bony nodules. To his touch it felt like chain mail. Could this be the skin from a giant sloth? He was astonished, and examined it with more care. The skin appeared so perfect it seemed as if the animal had died only yesterday. Excited, he made enquiries at the ranch. They told him it had come from deep inside a cave down by the sea; and that still other remains were there. He went to see. There were signs of human occupation and some animal droppings, which appeared quite fresh, and were large enough to have come from an elephant. He took some of the skin and the droppings back to Europe with him – hoping to be the first man to prove that the extinct giant sloth still existed, and was living in caves in Southern Patagonia. But the examination showed that the skin, the droppings, and the human remains were all thousands of years old. It was a mere accident that the atmosphere in the caves had been exactly right for preservation.

Later, other scientists went to explore the same caves and more interesting things came to light. They discovered that the remains of the animals were all at the far end of the cave cut off by a low wall. Nearby were some bales of hay and a kind of kitchen area, with sharp stone knives. So it seems that, way back in the past, the Indian tribes had kept huge animals very much like we keep cattle, penned behind a wall. They fed them hay to fatten them and then killed them by striking them on the skull – just as we slaughter animals.

Carbon-dating has proved that all the various remains in the Ultima Esperanza cave are about thirteen thousand years old. But that hasn't stopped people sending expedition after expedition to search this lonely area of South America to try to find that monster of Indian legend. A huge night-animal with an armoured fur-coat, "a wolf as big as a bull".

I don't know if they will ever find one, but I would like to be there to make a film of it if they do.

MERMAIDS
and other Marvels of the Sea

NE FRIDAY morn when we set sail,
Not very far from the land,
We there did espy a fair pretty maid,
With a comb and a glass in her hand.

I went on a search for mermaids – or merry-maids as they are called in Cornwall – and it took me to the lonely village of Zennor not far from Land's End. I didn't find a mermaid, but I found several stories about them. Often the stories have to do with music – it is said that when mermaids hear music they will come ashore to listen, and some even have taken on human shape so that they can join in at a village dance. You can always recognise a mermaid because the hem of her long dress will be still wet!

There is a story that once a mermaid lived among the rocks and caves of Zennor cove. Sometimes she could hear the sound of bells ringing from the church in the village up on the hill. So one day she came out of the sea, found her way up the stream and climbed to the church. She liked the sound of the service so much, and particularly the "sweet singing in the choir", that she visited the church over and over again. She always sat in the same bench, and after a time the villagers became quite used to her being there. Among the singers in the choir one young man called Matthew Trewella had a lovelier voice than the rest, and the mermaid fell in love with him. Eventually she persuaded him to come with her to the sea's edge. They disappeared together under the waves and were never seen again. Some years later a lobster fisherman anchored his boat near the cliffs and was busy pulling in his lobster-pots when up through the waves peered the familiar face of the Zennor mermaid. "Would you mind," she said, "you've got your anchor stuck right across the entrance to my cave. Matthew Trewella and I live here with our children, and the children are crying because they can't get out to play."

So the fisherman said he was sorry, pulled up his anchor and moved away. That was the last that was ever heard of Matthew Trewella and the mermaid of Zennor.

Zennor is very old, and the hills around it are littered with prehistoric buildings. In this part of Cornwall tin was mined long before the Romans came to Britain. Over two thousand years ago Mediterranean traders from far-distant Tyre and Sidon came in their sailing boats to buy valuable Cornish tin, and trade continued until early Christian times.

For the people of Zennor village the mermaid is still part of their daily life. The church is an old one – and an even older one was here before. It is a fisherman's church, and a boat that hangs from the ceiling is a memorial to men who have died at sea. A hundred years ago the inside of the church was full of heavy carved oak benches, but they have been replaced – all except one. That one has a mermaid carved on the end, a mermaid with a comb and a glass in her hand. It is supposed to be the bench where the mermaid used to sit. Not far away, in the next parish, there's a carving of Matthew Trewella who went to join her and live under the sea.

That is one of the nicer stories about mermaids – and there are many, many more. Some families in Ireland and in the Hebrides believe that among their ancestors they have a mermaid for a great-grandmother – and because of her the sea-people make sure that no member of the family can ever die by drowning.

There is a famous story of a family from the west coast of Ireland who owned a chapel by the edge of the sea – and for centuries all the family were buried there. Then in some fierce winter storm the sea covered up their graveyard, and the waves swept over the chapel. After that, when anyone died the coffin was carried down to the sea's edge, and the procession of mourners prayed over it and left it there. At night, on the full tide, the sea people would come up to collect the coffin and carry it down to be buried beneath the waves in the drowned chapel. It was said that one of their own kind had married into the family years before, and that was why they continued to perform this kindness.

Another family with a mermaid legend in its history once occupied the castle of the Counts of Luxembourg. The mermaid's name was Melusine and the condition of her marriage to a mortal husband was that he should never see her while she had her bath on Saturday afternoons, nor ask why, because then she turned back into a mermaid. Of course, one fatal Saturday afternoon the count, her husband, looked through the bathroom keyhole and saw her, mermaid's tail and all. Having discovered her secret he was about to creep quietly away when with an unearthly scream Melusine turned into a spirit and flew out of the window. She disappeared into a rock on which the city of Luxembourg now stands. And ever since she has been inside the rock knitting herself a new tail – one stitch every seven years for a thousand years.

There are many stories of mermaids begging to be allowed to be human. Hans Andersen's little mermaid died for the love of a human prince. Another mermaid fell in love with a monk from the monastery on Lindisfarne. She begged and wept so often to be given a human soul that her tears turned into the round green pebbles that the people of Lindisfarne still call mermaids' tears. Another mermaid was found in the lough near Belfast, and taken to church floating in a tank of water. There she was baptised a Christian and promptly died. There are many stories of mermaids singing such entrancing songs that seamen paid no attention to anything else and steered their ships onto the rocks and drowned. What is most interesting, though, is how long these stories have persisted and how widespread they are.

Pictures of mermen were still being shown among the pictures of real animals in the zoological dictionaries of the sixteenth- and seventeenth-centuries. They believed in other strange sea-people too, but for those who live near water and whose livelihood depends on fishing some half-human sea creature could easily become a sort of sea-god.

Chinese fishermen dance and bang gongs to keep the sea-gods away from their boats while they fish. The Red Indian tribes of North America have a legend that long ago they lived across the Pacific in another country. But the country was dry and barren and the tribe was starving. Then a man covered with fish-skin like a coat appeared swimming in the sea. He sang to them about

A "Sea Bishop" and a "Sea Monk" from a seventeenth-century book of natural history

the beauties of the undersea world and tried to persuade them to follow him under the water. When they refused he told them of another land far away across the sea where there was rich pasture and good hunting. If they followed him he would show them. So the Indians took to their boats and the singing sea-man piloted them across the ocean. After they had safely landed on the shores of America he disappeared into the sea, still singing. Another sea-god from ancient Babylon was said to have taught the humans how to behave during the day and returned to the sea every night.

But the tradition of mermaids seems quite different, they are much more human and less godlike. In 1824 a book was printed which was supposed to explain:

"Some account of the Merman now exhibiting at 174 Piccadilly – with observations on Mermaids and Mermen together with indubitable proof of their existence."

In the back of my copy there is a newspaper cutting which was stuck into the book later. It tells the story of a "Living Mermaid" put on show in Rome by an Englishman called Hudson ... "a most charming creature, half-woman, half-fish, reclining in an immense bath ... she appeared to have a sort of collar of fish scales and a tail which floated in the water with all the vitality of a real natural fish! But this bizarre creature spoke not a word – ever and anon she would open her mouth as if about to speak and then instantly plunge into the water ... the exhibition excited a lively curiosity and great enthusiasm". So much so, that one of the staff at the hotel where Mr Hudson was staying with his wonderful mermaid hid in his room and waited till the end of the show. He saw the Englishman drag the poor mermaid into his room by her fish-scale collar. She was shrieking for help – but the servant didn't understand English and thought she was speaking in her own sea-language. Then when he saw Hudson beating the poor creature he slipped away and fetched the police and Hudson was taken to court. The young woman who had played the mermaid's part was asked by the judge why she had never cried out for help while she was on public show – and she explained that she couldn't. There was a cord round her neck, and every time she opened her mouth to speak Hudson pulled the cord and she was plunged under the water in an instant. "The court sentenced Hudson to imprisonment for life. He heard his sentence with a smile and went out whistling an Irish Air."

I'm afraid many of the "indubitable proofs" in the book are of a similar nature. The mermaid displayed in

Piccadilly was "found on board a native vessel and carried to Batavia in a Dutch ship, where the present proprietor purchased it at a very considerable price."

The creature itself was of extreme ugliness, and the man who owned it seemed to know very little about it or its history – or allow anyone to get too close a look at it either. It was probably the body of a stuffed monkey joined to the tail of a large fish. From time to time other "real" mermaids have been put on show, yet not one has ever been proved genuine.

Yet the stories of mermaids persist and some have a ring of truth about them.

There were reports in the papers about a mermaid who was seen off the north coast of Scotland by several people, including a minister's daughter and the local schoolmaster. The descriptions are rather more real. "Only the face was visible. The sea at that time ran very high and as the waves advanced, the Mermaid sank under them, and afterwards re-appeared. The face was plump and round; the hair thick and long, of a green oily cast, and appeared troublesome to it ... as the wave retreated, with both its hands it frequently threw back the hair, the arms (one of them at least) frequently extended over its head, as if to frighten a bird that hovered over it and seemed to distress it much; when that had no effect, it sometimes turned quite round several times."

Many of the places – Lindisfarne, Cornwall, northern Scotland, Shetland, Ireland – where there are mermaid stories have large seal colonies. They swim, dive and turn with immense ease and grace. They are friendly, inquisitive creatures and they often surface in sight of a boat. Seals have their own collection of magic legends. On the Faroe islands it is said that every ninth night seals come ashore to dance ... and shed their skins to become human ... that if you can capture one and hide its skin it will remain human until it finds its own skin again ... that if you wear a piece of sealskin fur, the hairs of the fur will ruffle when the tide changes ... that seals can be charmed by music.

Certainly, seals, like many other of the large sea-going mammals, call to each other under water. The Eskimo hunters used to listen for their sounds by putting a wooden oar down beneath the water and using it as a sounding board. Could seals have been the original mermaids? It doesn't take a lot of imagination to read human feelings into their large friendly eyes.

Yet what about the long hair and the glass and comb? Perhaps some floating seaweed might account for mermaid's hair, but not the comb and the mirror. There is another sea animal just as friendly to man as the seal that could have connections with the legends – the dolphin. The ancient Greeks had many stories about dolphins – and in particular about dolphins which would come to the aid of men and carry them riding on their backs to land.

One of the stories was about a Greek singer who sang so beautifully that he won prizes in many countries and made a lot of money. As he was going home to his own Greek island, the sailors on his ship decided to murder him and steal the money. He begged to be allowed to sing once more before he died. They agreed, so he dressed in his most beautiful clothes and went up on deck to sing a long, sad, sacred song. The sailors were entranced, and didn't notice a dolphin swimming nearer and nearer the ship. Then suddenly the singer jumped overboard and the dolphin carried him on his back safely to his own home.

Then there are lots of stories of young Greek boys teaching dolphins to be their friends and take them on their backs while they went fishing. There are old coins which illustrate these stories and on some the boy is

Drawing of seals from the nineteenth-century

carrying a fishing trident and a shield – which look very like the mermaids' comb and mirror. Did the mermaids' comb and mirror travel to Cornwall with the tin-traders from Greece?

Perhaps the mermaid stories are a mixture of these two nice creatures, seals and dolphins, though some people suggest that the real mermaid was the poor old manatee, or sea-cow. Manatees live mostly in tropical seas and rivers and are not very beautiful. Certainly it would be hard to fall in love with one. Being a mammal, it is sometimes seen nursing its babies in its flippers like a human mother, which may explain why it is thought to have mermaid connections. Yet manatees live in warm waters and were never likely to have been seen off the north of Scotland. But there are more legendary marvels in the cold North Sea than mermaids.

"And there go eels, three hundred feet long and many other monsters, perilous and terrible – as dragons and

Olaus Magnus's drawing of a "Devil Fish"

serpents and other diverse beasts great and small."

One early naturalist was a Norwegian Bishop, Olaus Magnus, and he left behind drawings of some horrific sea-beasts which he believed inhabited the North Sea. They look like some seaman's nightmare, and for a long time they were considered as no more than myths from the middle ages and not taken seriously. But one at least, "the devil fish", has turned out to have some truth in it.

In 1802 a French writer gave a lurid account of a three-masted sailing ship that was attacked by a giant squid with arms thirty feet long; but it wasn't until the 1870s that zoologists began to believe fishermen's stories of a giant squid with immensely strong tentacles and eyes the size of saucers. Whalers had reported that they frequently found traces of whales having been attacked by enormous squids, and since then giant squids have been caught and photographed. Some have an overall length of thirty feet and would be quite capable of overturning a small boat, particularly if it had mistaken it for its natural enemy, the whale.

The common squid grows to only about six or seven inches overall – and it is small squids like these that you may have been offered to eat on holiday in Spain. The Spanish call them "callimares" and cook them with rice and other sea food – which makes a very good meal. Another fish which is common enough and has been eaten in this country for centuries, is the ordinary freshwater eel. It grows to about two feet long. If you have been fishing you might quite easily have caught one. But there is nothing ordinary about the life history of the eel – in fact their extraordinary life-cycle wasn't discovered until quite recently. It used to be thought that eels were sexless and grew spontaneously out of the mud of river beds. The exact story of the yearly journey of thousands of full-grown eels from the lakes and rivers of Europe to the mysterious Sargasso Sea – far away across the Atlantic – where they go to spawn, was only discovered by a Danish zoologist in the 1920s. The eel is born deep in mid-ocean. In their larval stage eels are glassy clear and only six inches long. These tiny leaf-like creatures are swept along in the warm gulf-stream, taking up to three years to reach European waters and begin to change into young eels. Young eels – elvers –

Artist's impression of giant octopus attacking a ship

arrive at the coasts of Europe in the spring determined to reach the inland lakes and streams. A young eel will wriggle through or over or under anything in order to get up-stream to its feeding grounds. In the spring thousands of them are seen hurrying inland – country people call it the "eel fair". But basically they are nocturnal animals, and on cold nights will hide away in mud to keep from frosts.

As soon as they are fully matured, which may take six or seven years, they start their journey back to the Sargasso Sea – this time without stopping even to eat on the way. They travel all the way back to the ocean in one short winter to breed and spawn, and presumably after that to die, because they are never seen again. They start this last "sea-run" in the autumn and it is then that whole colonies of silvery eels have been seen travelling at night – even crossing roads, in their compulsion to get back to the sea.

There is still a lot more to be discovered about different kinds of eels. One, the Moray eel, does not leave the sea at all. It has been called the scourge of skin-divers, because it lives among coral reefs and is said to attack divers with its strong teeth and powerful jaws. But how many more species of eel there might be fathoms deep in the oceans of the world, no one yet knows. For instance, among the specimens of larval eels which the Danish zoologist who first discovered them brought back from the Sargasso Sea, one was six feet long. It makes one wonder if this could be the larval stage of a giant adult eel? If a six-inch larva becomes two feet long when grown, you might think that a six-foot larva could grow twenty-four feet long. But simple arithmetic is not always correct in the world of natural history. Even so, it could be the clue to the many stories of giant sea-serpents.

In modern times probably the most famous of the

sea-serpents was seen in 1817 off the coast of North America, near the harbour of Gloucester. It seems to have been seen by literally hundreds of people who swore evidence before a Justice of the Peace.

"I Matthew Allen of Gloucester, Ship's Carpenter, depose and say: that on the fourteenth day of August 1817 I saw a strange marine animal, resembling a serpent. I was in a boat, and was within thirty feet of him."

"I, Solomon Allen of Gloucester, Shipmaster, depose and say: that I have seen a strange marine animal, that I believe to be a serpent, in the harbour in the said Gloucester. I would judge him to be between eighty and ninety feet in length."

Thirty years later a British Naval captain and some of the crew of HMS *Daedalus* reported to the Admiralty that in the South Atlantic they had encountered a sea-serpent more than sixty feet long. They watched the creature for a full twenty minutes. In his formal letter to

Drawing of a sea-serpent reported near Gloucester, USA

Impression of the sea-serpent when first seen from HMS *Daedalus*

the Admiralty the captain wrote: "I am having a drawing of the serpent made from a sketch, which I hope to have ready for my Lords Commissioners of the Admirality by tomorrow's post". If only they had had a camera, perhaps more people would have believed them. As it was, they were dismissed as mere "romantics" who had imagined a ghost ... as was everyone else who reported they had seen a serpent in the sea. In fact a Captain Cringle who reported seeing a sea-serpent in 1893 was laughed at so much that he said he wished he had never mentioned it. But here is his report in the ship's log:

"HMS *Umfuli*. Monday, December 4th 1893. 2pm – calm and smooth sea. 4pm – same weather. 5.30pm – sighted and passed about five hundred yards from the ship a monster fish of the serpent shape, about eighty feet long with slimy skin and short fins. In shape it was just like a conger eel."

On that voyage there *was* a man with a camera, but he was so excited just watching the monster that he forgot to go and get his camera. The same mixture of interest and sneering disbelief has been shown to every story about the Loch Ness Monster. It is a story that first hit the newspapers in the 1930s. In July 1933 George Spicer and his wife who were on holiday in Scotland, were driving by the edge of Loch Ness. It was mid-afternoon and the light was good. Suddenly Mrs Spicer shouted. A dark grey trunk-like thing shot across the road in front of them, followed by a revolting slug-like body. It quite filled the road. A huge animal slithered down the hillside, crossed the road and disappeared into the loch below. Mr Spicer saw traces of its track through the bracken.

Since then the deep waters of Loch Ness have been continuously searched and watched. The monster – if that is what it is – has been photographed many times, from the air, from the shore, and from a few feet away. Some short pieces of film have been taken. There have been innumerable sworn statements by people who say they have seen it both in the water and on land by the edge of the Loch.

Nevertheless, the Loch Ness Monster is still thought of as half a joke and the people who see it are only half-believed. Could it be some kind of giant eel? Eels are nocturnal creatures which can hide in deep mud, and they have been seen on land. Young eels always seem to return to the same feeding grounds. They do not like the cold and Loch Ness is one of the few Scottish lakes that has never been known to freeze.

For centuries, long before 1933, Loch Ness already had a reputation as the home of monsters. It might be possible that some giant eels have returned there from time to time to feed in this freshwater lake; even sometimes travelling overland, like their smaller cousins. It is a possible theory.

But there are people who have made long studies of Loch Ness who believe that if there is a creature there at all, it is a surviving reptile from hundreds of millions of years ago. Perhaps it is a Plesiosaurus or similar giant reptile. The difficulty about that theory is that a reptile would have to come up to breathe at least once every half-hour or so and so would have been seen more often.

Yet it is possible that it is some sort of surviving pre-historic creature. Only a short while ago, a fossil fish, the Coelacanth, which was thought to have become extinct seventy million years ago, was found to be alive and well living in the seas near the African coast – so you never know. There is still so much to be discovered in the vast depths of the sea that it would be a foolish man who would say that sea-monsters don't exist.

DRAGONS & SERPENTS

 MONG all the kinds of serpents there is none comparable to the Dragon — or that affordeth and yieldeth so much plentiful matter in history ... for the ample discovery of their Nature.

That was written over three hundred years ago by an Englishman called Edward Topsell. He wrote an animal book which was immensely popular in its day. It was based on a much larger set of volumes for scholars of natural history which had been written in Latin. Topsell's book was called: *A History of Four-Footed Beasts and Serpents*.

Among the chapters describing quite ordinary animals like tigers and cats, zebras and monkeys, there is a chapter about serpents including a section on dragons. In those days dragons, serpents, and something they called the boas were all very much muddled up and all considered equally terrible. Topsell himself was quite confused about the differences between dragons and serpents: "The dragons get and hide themselves in trees, covering their heads and letting the other part hang down like a rope. They watch till the elephant comes and then do they clasp themselves about his neck and beat and vex the elephant until they strangle him."

In the jungle very large snakes like pythons and boas can drop on their prey from trees – though scarcely in such a dramatic manner – nor would they get very far with an attack on an elephant. But the world of the real jungle was so far away from the scholars of Europe. Snakes, serpents, and flying dragons were all reptiles and all fearsome. And perhaps they had heard strange

stories from the East. In the past, to Europeans the East was full of jungles, and jungles were full of serpents, and after all dragons were only another kind of serpent. From the East came all the most wonderful stories of strange gods, rare jewels and fearful monsters.

Marco Polo had said that in India there was a kingdom of mountains "where in all the world diamonds are found and nowhere else". And those diamond-bearing mountains were infested with immense serpents that lived in dark caves and were exceedingly venomous and noxious.

So serpents became a symbol of fear. They lived in dark holes and they came to represent darkness and evil. People from Britain and the northern countries had never seen any large snakes, they had only heard stories, and so they had to make do with imaginary serpents. Dragons and serpents, poisonous reptiles and the devil were all intertwined and all mysterious, and like giants and monsters they made good stories.

In Yorkshire near Whitby there was once an old and very famous abbey. It was first started in the seventh century by the daughter of a king, whose name has come down to us as St Hilda. She ran the abbey and two monasteries – one for men, and one for women – and seems to have been a very powerful person.

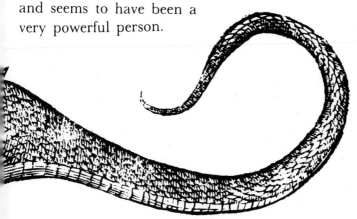

But there is one odd story told about her which says that the grounds of the abbey at Whitby were infested by hundreds of serpents. Then St Hilda prayed, and at once the snakes turned into stone. To complete their destruction their heads dropped off. Of course, you will recognise that the headless stone serpents were really fossils – the ancient petrified sea-creatures called ammonites. You can dig them up in various parts of England, just as you can find fossil shells, fossil sea-urchins, and other remains where the land was once part of the sea-bed, millions of years ago. Now we know something about fossils, but once it must have been only too easy to link them with the legends about St Hilda.

Before the real origin of fossils was known they were collected just as curiosities – as stone bones. Some people found them so strange and beautiful they were used as magic charms, against thunderstorms, seasickness, witchcraft and poison. Fossil sharks' teeth were sometimes made into jewellery. They were called "tongue-stones" or "St Paul's Stones". Wearing one round your neck would protect you in battle, or even make you irresistible to women! It was said that a glass of wine into which one of these fossil teeth had been dipped would cure any sickness.

In China fossil teeth were known sometimes as dragon's teeth – in fact they were probably mostly teeth of extinct apes and horses. But right up until recent times, in the valley of the Shansi river the peasants would work on their farms in the summer, and dig for dragon's teeth in the winter. Once a year men from the cities would come and buy the harvest of dragon's teeth by the pound, take them back to their medicine shops, and pulverise them and sell them in powder form as a wonderful magical cure.

This trade in dragon's teeth can be traced right back to the fifth century and still exists today in parts of

Hong Kong and Borneo. I know because I have bought a so-called dragon's tooth in a Chinese medicine shop in Borneo.

Chinese dragons were much nicer than western ones. They were considered a good luck symbol and were meant to live among the clouds in the sky and bring the rain. Their voices were said to be like gongs sounding. In most Chinese communities, once a year they hold a Dragon Festival. It is like a carnival, and men dress up as huge paper dragons and parade along the streets. The children rush around throwing buckets of water at everyone and shouting "Here comes the rain!" Perhaps it was this friendly eastern dragon that Edward Topsell had in mind when he wrote: "There are Dragons of sundry colours and their shape and outward appearance is very beautiful. Some are black, some red, some of an ash colour and some yellow."

Of course some people think the crocodile could have been the dragon. They are fierce and horrible enough! But there was never anything particularly mysterious about crocodiles. Even in ancient days a lot was known about them – they were known as the egg-breeding serpents. "Now a crocodile is like a lizard in all points (excepting the tail and the size of the lizard) yet it layeth an Egge no greater than a goose's egg, and from so small a beginning ariseth this monstrous serpent. The biting of the crocodile is very sharp, deep and deadly, so that wheresoever he layeth his teeth, seldom or never followeth any cure. The tail is the strongest part; they never kill any beast or man but first of all they strike him down and astonish him with their tails. And therefore the Egyptians did sygnify death and darkness by a Crocodile's tail."

The Egyptians made gods of their Nile crocodiles. Their temple priests would decorate them with gold bracelets on their paws and jewels on their heads.

The Romans, too, knew all about them. Their soldiers went hunting on the River Nile, and the Emperor Tiberius Caesar had one as a pet and fed it by hand. No one ever seems to have got crocodiles confused with the legendary dragons. But in some of the old Roman histories they talk of another kind of crocodile. They describe it merely as a giant land crocodile – a lizard.

It was more modern stories of an unknown giant lizard that lived in a remote part of the East Indies that once set me off on a hunt for what I hoped was a live dragon.

In 1910 there had been reports of a large flesh-eating lizard from an island near Java called Komodo. It is a tiny island almost in the middle of the Indonesian archipelago, and why the giant lizard should exist there is a problem no one has solved. The native people said the lizards live in caves deep in the heart of the island, and are very dangerous, eating deer, pig and even humans. In the 1920s an airman whose plane was forced down came face to face with one of these beasts. He said it was huge – like a dragon. Several European

explorers visited the island, some to shoot the dragons and some to bring specimens home for zoos.

In 1956 I set off with a cameraman to try to put the dragons of Komodo onto film. When we reached the island, we were told that the dragons have a keen sense of smell and that the best way to attract them would be to bait a trap with goat meat. We constructed a ten-foot long box trap open at one end, baited it with goat meat, and hung more meat from a nearby tree so that the smell would spread widely. We waited in hiding, enduring for an hour or so the stench of the rotting meat only fifteen yards away. It was then I heard a rustle behind me, and turning round, found myself facing a Komodo dragon.

He was enormous. From the tip of his narrow head to the end of his long keeled tail I guessed he measured over ten feet. He was so close that I could see every beady scale in his hoary black skin. He was standing high on his four bowed legs, his heavy body lifted clear of the ground, his head erect and menacing. From his half-closed jaws an enormous yellow-pink forked tongue flicked in and out.

The soft whirring of the film-camera seemed almost deafening to us, but the creature was not concerned and watched us imperiously with his unblinking black eye. It was as though he realised he was the most powerful beast on Komodo, and that, as king of the island, he feared no other creature. Just then a young dragon no more than three feet long approached the bait on the tree. This one had much brighter markings, its tail banded with dark rings and its forelegs and shoulders spotted with flecks of dull orange. It walked briskly with a peculiar gait, twisting its spine sideways and wriggling its hips, savouring the smell of the bait with its long yellow tongue. The dragon behind us emitted a deep sigh, flexed its legs and slowly stalked round us.

41

Another enormous dragon approached the bait, and soon three of the creatures were tearing at the goat's flesh right in front of us. The biggest beast was so large that it could carry the complete leg of a full-grown goat in its mouth.

When I took a cautious step outside the hide the dragons continued feeding without so much as a glance in my direction. I was able to photograph them from only six feet away. Eventually, one of the dragons scented the bait inside the box trap. Slowly he went inside to investigate. Suddenly the spring worked and the trap door came sharply down. I had caught my first dragon.

I was not able to bring him back to England, so after examining him, I let him go. But if I *hadn't* been able to make a film of my expedition; if I'd just come home and told my dragon story and other people had told more dragon stories about *my* story, perhaps that giant lizard might have developed into a dragon like St George's dragon.

St George's story has been told so many times it is hard to discover if there was ever any truth in it at all.

"In a certain country they suffered exceedingly from the attacks of a fierce and insatiable dragon. Each year it demanded a sacrifice until at last the time came when it demanded the king's daughter for its victim. Fearfully, the princess went to meet her fate. It was then that a Christian knight came to her rescue. He told the princess to take the girdle from her waist and place it round the dragon's neck and then the beast would not harm her. She led the dragon back into the city and there in front of all the people St George fought and killed the dragon."

The English armies of the crusades brought back that legend from the East and over the years St George became a battle cry for other English armies, until eventually he became St George of England. There is some doubt about whether St George ever existed, but perhaps his dragon was some fairy-tale version of a creature like the Komodo dragon.

Topsell's book lists yet another kind of dragon. He calls it the Fire Dragon, and says: "It destroys the fruits of the earth with a certain burning fire in the air, and sometimes on the Sea and Land. Which it did twelve

The flesh-eating "dragon" lizard from Komodo

years ago on the Western Seas, on the coasts of England."

That was written in 1658, but in 1973 on the coasts of Iceland another "certain burning fire in the air destroyed many of the fruits of the earth", when the new volcano of Heimaye island suddenly burst into life. The old stories of Icelandic heroes often describe a sleeping dragon that lives underground and suddenly wakens with an earth-shattering roar to lay waste the surrounding land – like the dragon in the story of Beowulf.

"The creature began to spew fire and burn dwellings; the light of the burning filled people with horror and the flying monster spared no living thing. It surrounded the country with fire and flame and burning and then flew back to its secret hideout. Filled with anger, Beowulf set out to find the dragon. He caught sight of its cavern full of swirling flame and shouted out his challenge. The dragon roared with rage at the sound of the man's voice. Its scorching breath spurted out from the grey rock. The prince stood his ground in the shelter of his great shield while the flaming monster hurtled towards him. Beowulf struck at the glittering dragon with his sword, but his blade failed. The dragon took fresh heart, and spitting flame, he ended Beowulf's life. But when day broke the dragon that had killed him lay there crushed and lifeless."

The firemen on Heimeye island fought the fires from their volcano in much the same way, though during the volcanic eruption of 1973 no one was killed. But even though we can now predict the movements of volcanoes and when and where they are likely to come to life, we still need to know more. Each new eruption is a battleground for more scientific knowledge – and as Topsell might have said: "A more ample discovery of the nature of fire dragons."

WINGED CREATURES

*OT KNOWING what to do, I gazed out over the land and far away beheld something white. As I approached it I thought it to be a white dome and found it to be very smooth. Then, all of a sudden the sky became dark and I was much astonished when I saw a bird* of monstrous size, and I realised the great dome must be its egg. I remembered that I had heard mariners speak of such a miraculous bird which they called the Roc. Its legs were as big as the trunk of a tree. That night I tied myself to one of its legs and the next day it flew away with me and carried me to a high mountain.

That comes from the story of Sinbad the sailor. His account of the miraculous bird was one of many Arab folk-tales brought back to Europe by the armies of the Crusaders in the middle ages. It was a time of exploration and adventure, and of "travellers' tales". When Marco Polo went on his immensely long journey from Venice across Asia to China and the court of Kublai Khan, he heard more stories of a huge rare bird – "so big", he was told, "and with legs so strong that its kick can fell an ox. It is known as the Rukh, and it will even seize an elephant and carry him on high". He was shown two enormous eggs to convince him of the bird's existence, and two huge feathers sixty feet long, which were probably only dried up palm-tree leaves. All the same Marco Polo believed in the elephant bird and said that it was to be found to the south of the island of Madagascar. There were many other travellers' tales written at that time and some of them were obviously full of tall stories, so that Madagascar and Marco Polo's elephant-bird were half-forgotten. Then, three hundred years later when the French first took command of part of the island of Madagascar, to use as a base for their ships trading with India, Admiral Etienne de Flacourt was made Governor. In 1658 he wrote a book about the new island territory. It is a fairly full account of the people and their customs, and de Flacourt makes a list of the island's plants and animals. He describes a wild ass with long floppy ears, an ape with a round face like a man's, and then: "There is a giant bird that lives in the south of the Island. It seeks the most lonely places and is rarely seen because it is shy and timid. It is a kind of ostrich.. The local people use the eggs to carry water, as I have seen myself."

During the next two hundred years, parts of these enormous eggs were found and sent back to France. The natives of Madagascar still used the egg-shells to carry water, but said they were very precious and hard to find because the bird that laid them was hardly ever seen; it lived only in the deepest jungle. Then, in 1866 a French naturalist discovered the bones of a huge unknown animal – they proved to belong to a bird nearly nine feet high. The bones were not fossilised –

but came from a creature that had existed until quite recently, and like the dodo had become extinct. The bird was larger and heavier than an ostrich with legs like tree trunks. And eggs, or fragments of them, were still to be found. The bird was given the name Aepyornis maximus, meaning, the largest of the tall birds. At last there was proof that Marco Polo's giant bird of Madagascar had really existed, and even though its wings were never strong enough for it to fly, its eggs were certainly of giant size – the largest known to science.

A few years ago I went on an expedition to Madagascar. I had read all the stories about the elephant bird and I was determined to find at least a small fragment of one of those legendary eggs.

The southern part of Madagascar is now a desert of dry sand, blindingly white, and so hot that it seems as if little could exist there. The climate of the island has undergone dramatic changes, and it is likely that when the giant bird lived it was not desert at all. I found a dried-up river bed nearly a mile wide which carries a stream of water only during the rainy season. When the Aepyornis was alive the desert was probably a great area of swamp. Searching among the pebbles on the river bed I found tiny pieces of egg-shell nearly a quarter of an inch thick. I had little hope of finding a whole egg, for of course most eggs are broken by the chick as it hatches, and only the rare addled ones remain whole. But if I could find just one large piece, I would have some idea of the actual size of the originals.

I searched the rest of that day without any more success, but I tried in my bad French to explain my peculiar quest to a young native boy who appeared, obviously mystified as to why I was grovelling about in the desert miles away from anywhere. Next morning I had a visitor. A woman came to the camp bringing hundreds of the egg fragments that I had thought so rare. They had been collected within a radius of only a few miles, and I must have been blind not to find more myself. But all the pieces were tiny. More basket loads of egg fragments were delivered to the camp all day long. Then, in the evening, the boy re-appeared. Carefully wrapped up in a handkerchief he produced some really large pieces of egg-shell, which, miraculously, looked as though they might all fit together. I laid the pieces out on the ground as though I were doing a jig-saw puzzle and began work, using adhesive tape. With mounting excitement I managed to get piece after piece to fit. At the end of an hour I had two complete halves, and to my joy they fitted together perfectly. I had found a whole Aepyornis egg, which is still one of my most precious possessions. Was this the egg that started Sinbad's story – this, what Marco Polo wondered at seven hundred years ago at the court of Kublai Khan? It is as big as a hundred and fifty chicken's eggs – and if it were used as a water-carrier, it could hold more than a gallon.

The roc or Aepyornis may have been the heaviest and largest bird that we know, but a very similar sort of bird was even taller, up to twelve feet. It is known as the moa, and once lived in New Zealand. But when the Maori tribes first arrived there these large birds were an important source of food for them. Unfortunately, they hunted them to death.

The bird that everyone knows best as "dead" is the poor silly dodo (its latin name Didus ineptus means literally that). The early Portuguese explorers were the first Europeans to see the dodo. They were seeking a safe sea-route to India and discovered the island of Mauritius half-way across the Indian Ocean – the perfect base for their ships to restock with water and food. There, much to their amusement, were hundreds

Artist's impression of the giant bird of Madagascar, Aepyornis maximus

of these weird and wonderful birds – unable to fly, and easy to catch for food. For a hundred years, European trading ships stopped at Mauritius and the neighbouring island of Reunion, and the sailors amused themselves hunting among the flocks of fat and harmless dodos. One sailor wrote: "We call them the disgusting birds, because the longer their flesh is cooked the more disgusting it becomes!" But this certainly did not stop them being eaten. Another sailor reported:

"From March to September the birds are very fat and exceptionally tasty".

Like parrots and monkeys, a few of the funny-looking dodos were brought back to Europe as traveller's souvenirs. No one had seen anything like them before, and to have a dodo in your zoo – or even a painting of one in your castle – was a status symbol in the royal courts of seventeenth-century Europe. But no one took much interest in the birds themselves, or in their welfare. Dodos were a joke, and anyway, according to the sailors, the islands were full of them. Then suddenly it dawned on European zoologists that there were fewer and fewer reports about dodos. Indeed, within a mere hundred years from their first discovery, all the birds had been destroyed. In the whole world not a single

Engraving of a dodo

dodo was left. The only record of their existence was a handful of paintings and one single stuffed specimen. This stuffed bird was on exhibition in an Oxford museum, and you would think it was something to be treasured very carefully. But not at all. In 1775, the museum governors were busy spring-cleaning and thought their stuffed dodo looked a bit moth-eaten. There and then they gave orders for it to be destroyed. So the last surviving remains of the dodo were thrown away; except for its head and one foot which some wise person decided to keep.

Since then, with the help of the paintings and a few old bones, good models of the dodo have been made by museums, but those eighteenth-century museum directors in Oxford so keen to spring-clean have gone down forever in the black-books of museum history.

None of these large half-legendary birds was able to fly. The only birds with wings large enough to cause a shadow across the sun like Sinbad's bird would have been the South American condor. Bigger than the eagle, it is the largest of all flying birds, and lives high in the Andes mountains. Its wing spread covers nine feet, and it feeds on carrion and even on young goats and lambs. It is so large and unwieldy that when it has fed well, it cannot manage to fly very high. Like our own magnificent golden eagle, the condor is often unnecessarily killed. People are afraid of birds of prey, although they admire their strength and beauty.

There are many old legends about large flying birds. Probably the oldest and most mysterious of these fabulous creatures is the rare and beautiful phoenix. A bird of fantasy: "in all the world there is only one", so the story goes. In the time of the Roman Emperors, Pliny wrote: "one was put on show in Rome, but I think it was a fictitious phoenix only!" Its story was already ancient and only half-believed. The phoenix was supposed to be as big as an eagle, with feathers of fine gold, azure blue and red. Every five hundred years – so it was said – the phoenix flew away to a lonely mountain on the coast of Arabia – to Phoenicia in fact. There, on a special high tree, near a cool fountain, it built its nest out of aromatic twigs and then, singing its last song it beat its wings rapidly in the sun and caused the nest to catch fire till everything, nest and bird itself, was consumed by the perfumed flames. Three days later, out of the cooling ashes, sprang another identical full-grown phoenix – and so again in all the world, there was only one phoenix.

Stories of these magical half-sacred birds have come down to us, in one form or another, from Arabia, from China and particularly from the Egypt of the Pharaohs. But the ancient Egyptians had many other bird gods. The sacred ibis was a bird that poured the waters of life out from a vase. It is actually a kind of stork that comes from the mountains surrounding the head-waters of the River Nile. Horus, the god of the upper air, is a high-flying falcon who wears the sun as a crown – a symbol of the pharaoh's own crown of Egypt. There were also heavenly geese whose cry first broke the silence of the dawn of the world and from whose first egg the sun was said to have been born. The goddess of the dead was the sacred vulture. These were all real birds, used by the Egyptians as symbols of life and death.

In those ancient days, soothsayers used to try to read omens from the flight of birds. The way a particular bird flew before a battle could mean good or bad fortune. A trace of that tradition is still with us, when we take a chicken's "wish-bone" and pull it apart. It used to be said whoever won the larger piece would have good fortune in the coming battle. Magic and birds have always been closely connected. The chariot horses of the gods, magic bulls, and even baby cherubs,

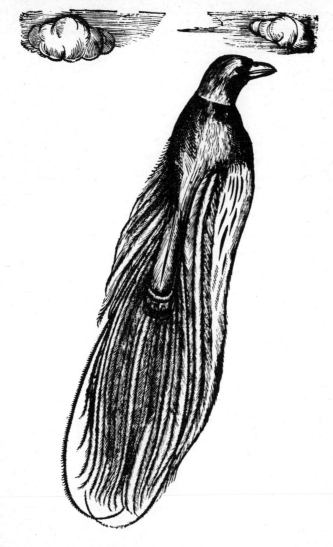

Seventeenth-century drawing of a bird of paradise feeding on dews of heaven

once given wings all seem to become magical heavenly creatures.

There are also some very real birds which were once quite seriously thought to have come straight from heaven, and are still known as birds of paradise. They come from New Guinea, and they are extraordinarily beautiful, and some people suppose that is how they got their name. But the real story is quite different.

In 1522 when Magellan's sailors – the first ever to sail right round the world – landed in the Spice Islands, they were given some rare bird skins by the Sultan of the islands. They were skins of birds of paradise, and the sailors brought them back to Europe. The bird skins had been carefully preserved with their legs and wings removed, so that the gorgeous coloured plumes sprouting from beneath the wings were seen to their greatest advantage. When these skins were examined in Europe the story got around that unlike ordinary and plainer birds, these rare creatures had no legs, but lived in heaven feeding on dew, and when they died they fell straight from the sky to earth. God's birds, they were called. The Portuguese sailors who had brought the bird skins home as trophies, explained that this wasn't true, but nobody wanted to know. And so the story grew and grew and was believed right up until the nineteenth century.

Alfred Wallace was the first man to bring back two of these birds alive. He brought them to the zoo in London, and then everyone could see that they had legs like any other bird. While searching for the birds in New Guinea, Wallace kept a diary: "The feelings of a naturalist who at last sees with his own eyes a creature of such extraordinary beauty and rarity would require the touch of a poet. I found myself on a remote island, far from the routes of merchant fleets; wandered through luxuriant tropical forests ... and here, I gazed upon the bird of paradise, the quintessence of beauty. I thought of the vanished ages during which generation after generation of birds lived and died – in dark gloomy forests, where no intelligent eye beheld their loveliness. And I wondered at this lavish squandering of beauty."

HORNS OF MAGIC

*HE KEEPER did a-hunting go —
Under his cloak he carried a bow
All for to shoot the merry little doe
Among the leaves so green o!*

For centuries, wild deer roamed the forests and hills of Europe. In Britain, in the middle ages, they were considered the property of the King and were free to go where they wished. Hunting them was a strictly royal privilege. If the rich barons wanted to enclose a herd within their own land they had to have royal permission first and pay a royal price for it, too. Only outlaws like Robin Hood stole deer for its meat.

Stag hunting – unlike some other forms of hunting – at least provides eatable meat. Hunters, though, often take great pride in killing the master stag – the one with the most splendid horns. There is an old legend about a Roman general who was keen on stag hunting. He had spent the day chasing a magnificent animal with ten points on its antlers. At last, when he had the beast cornered and was about to shoot it, a shaft of evening light shone through its horns and a voice said: "I am Christ, why do you pursue me?" So the general didn't make the kill, but became a Christian instead. In fact he became a Saint – Saint Eustacius. He was always known as the patron saint of hunters, although it might have been nicer to be the patron saint of hunted stags! In the old books of the middle ages the stag was often said to represent Christians. One of them says: "These creatures are enemies to serpents. When they feel themselves weighed down by sickness, they suck snakes from their holes in the ground with a snort from the nostrils. After eating the snakes, they shed their coats and all their old age with them. Similarly, when Christians snuff up the devil-snake sin, they run with confession to our Lord Jesus Christ and are then renovated – their Old Age of Sin having been shed."

Stags don't eat snakes – they feed on grass and young shoots. But they are one of the horned animals that seem to have collected many odd legends, and hunting and collecting horns as trophies goes back a long way before Christian times.

Every year on the first Sunday of September in the village of Abbots Bromley in Staffordshire a very ancient ceremony is played out. Six men wearing huge horns on their heads – three with black masks and three with white – dance their way for twenty miles around the boundaries of the village. It is a quaint old village custom, but the dance must go back to the ancient pagan fertility rites of harvest time. The horns are reindeer horns, and are said to be at least a thousand years old. They came, like the Vikings, from Scandinavia. The black and white masks symbolise the fight between light and dark – between winter and spring – which was a vital part of the Viking mythology.

But the idea of wearing the horns of the animal being hunted is not only a magical practice, it can have a practical purpose too. Red Indian hunters dressed in the skins of buffalo or deer could get within easy bow-shot of their prey without being detected.

In Britain the largest of the native wild deer is the red deer. An adult red deer stands four feet high and its antlers can be three feet across. Deer antlers, unlike the horns of other animals, are solid horn, and every year in spring they are cast – dropped off – and a fresh set of horns grows – bigger and better ones each year.

When newly-grown the antlers are covered in a soft skin – known as velvet. In the late summer this starts to wear off, and the animals rub the velvet against trees and on the ground to harden their horns for fighting. Perhaps these tatters of summer velvet were mistaken for serpents in the old days. By the time all the velvet is off, the deer are fighting fit. For most of the year the males and the females live apart, but in the autumn when the breeding season starts the adult males fight to decide which will be master. There is a lot of bellowing, and crashing and banging – and the fights can last up to half-an-hour. But it is a show of strength, rather than a fight to the death. The strongest wins the right to all the females, but he has to keep on bellowing, just to make sure the others continue to recognise he is king.

Tinkers used to make spoons and beakers out of deer horns. Some people still claim that medicine taken from a horn spoon or drunk from a horn cup is better for you. Once, people believed that powdered deer-horn mixed with grease and rubbed on to a sprain was a sure magical cure. And it was said that burning deer-horns was powerful magic to keep snakes away.

The connection between animals and magic goes back as far into history as we know – primitive men painted the walls of their caves with pictures of animals which seem to be more than just simple portraits. They may have belonged to some magic ritual – a way to get the gods to increase the number of animals for hunting and the strength of the men who hunted them.

Of all the animals they painted, the huge wild bull takes pride of place. When Julius Caesar first wrote about the tribes living in the forests of Germany he wrote about the German auroch – a wild black bull: "Nearly as large as an elephant, though in shape and colour resembling a bull. They are of uncommon strength and swiftness, and spare neither man nor beast that comes in their way. They are hunted chiefly by the young men. They preserve the horns with great care, decorating the rims with silver and at their most solemn festivals they drink from them instead of cups".

During the next one thousand five hundred years these huge wild bulls were hunted mercilessly. By the sixth century in France only the royal hunt had the right to kill them.

By the time the sixteenth-century zoologists were listing the known animals of the world, there were only thirty of the great aurochs left, living in the forests of

Hunting the auroch.

Lithuania. One by one they died off, and within fifty years not one of these huge black European cattle existed, although their bones and huge horns are still dug up in various parts of Europe and Britain. In this country it was often white cattle that were killed by the young men at solemn festivals. White bulls with black horns and red ears were known by the Welsh poets as "fairy cattle" or magic cattle.

Two thousand years ago when Julius Caesar's Roman soldiers came to Britain they brought with them some of their religious beliefs. One of them was the worship of a Persian god – Mithras. It seems to have been some kind of secret religion. Underground temples to Mithras have been found wherever the conquering Roman armies settled. The symbol of Mithras was a white bull which was ceremonially stabbed to death by a young man. From its blood new crops were expected to grow. Several Mithraic temples were found along the great wall which the Romans built across the northern counties of England, and not long ago one was discovered under the City of London when a new office block was being built.

In the Cheviot Hills – where traces of other Roman camps still remain to be explored – is the last herd of wild white cattle of Britain. Perhaps they are the last of a herd specially bred for sacrifice to Mithras.

An old description of the white bulls of the border country says: "They had such hatred against the society and company of men, that they eat not of the herbs that were touched or handled by men. Though they seem meek and tame, they are more wild than any other beasts."

Several hundred years ago the owners of Chillingham castle were given royal permission to enclose the wild cattle inside their park, and they have remained there ever since; quite untamed.

The Chillingham cattle do not like people – they do not even like the smell of people – and will form up in a semi-circle and charge anyone foolish enough to go in among them. The Chillingham herd today is in the care of a warden, but they are still wild animals. They live as a wild herd, with their own herd laws and herd rules. They have a king bull who leads them and is responsible for breeding. He has to fight his way to be king and will remain in charge until he is eventually challenged and defeated by a younger and stronger bull. No one ever touches a calf, even if it is sick, or the rest of the herd will turn against it and kill it.

In 1790 the British naturalist Thomas Bewick visited the Chillingham cattle. He was writing and illustrating a book, and described a bull hunt at Chillingham: "The mode of killing them was perhaps, the only modern remains of the grandeur of ancient hunting. On notice being given that a wild bull would be killed on a certain day, the inhabitants of the neighbourhood came

Thomas Bewick's engraving of the Chillingham bull

mounted, and armed with guns, sometimes to the amount of a hundred horsemen, and four or five hundred on foot, who stood on the walls, or got into the trees, while the horsemen rode off the Bull from the rest of the herd, until he stood at bay; then a marksman dismounted and shot; to the shouts of savage joy echoing from every side!" Bewick was not able to draw the reigning king bull of his day because, he said, he was unable to get near to it. Instead he portrayed a defeated king. One of the last of the bull hunts took place in 1872 when the young man who was to become Edward VII shot a Chillingham bull with a rifle.

A different sort of bull-hunt still takes place in Spain. It used to be said that white bulls were sacrificed to the good gods and black bulls to the evil ones. The fierce fighting bulls of Spain don't look so very different from the wild cattle of Britain. They may appear small but their horns are just as deadly. Ceremonial fighting of bulls seems to be a ritual that goes back into the distant past. The earliest picture of a Spanish bull-fight is in the thirteenth century. It may have been brought to Spain by the Romans.

Long before the Romans sacrificed bulls to their gods, in ancient Greece, Egypt and Crete, bulls were brought garlanded to different altars, sometimes to be worshipped, sometimes to be sacrificed. In Crete, the bull was a sacred animal. Among the splendid remains of King Minos' palace in Crete a bull-horn altar was discovered, and many bull statues, paintings, and decorated cups.

For centuries, the people of the East have connected cattle with religious practices. In the Nile valley when a sacred cow died it was buried in the ground with just its horns protruding from the earth. Today, for Moslems and Hindus, the flesh of cattle is forbidden food. If this seems difficult to understand, think how shocked we are at the thought of eating horses. Yet the food-value of horse-flesh is quite good. Once upon a time the horse was a sacred animal in Britain, and the huge pictures of white horses drawn on our chalk-downs are traces of that belief. Even now, we still treat horses with something of the respect of ancient gods. At horse shows we stick garlands on them – and we would have to be very hungry indeed before we would think of eating them.

There is one horned creature more fabulous than the rest – the unicorn. The unicorn was supposed to be a rare and admirable beast which was hardly ever seen because it lived alone on the edge of the world. It had a single horn on its forehead and was beautiful, like a white horse, but strong, fierce and quite untameable. The way to catch one was to take a young maiden into the forest and leave her there alone. When the wild unicorn scented her presence, he would come quietly and lay his head in her lap, and allow himself to be caught. Then the hunters would take him to the king's palace, where they cut off his horn by force and sent him away alive.

That story started with the Greeks and Romans, and was repeated again and again and more or less believed throughout the middle ages. It was a favourite fable, but one that was always being questioned. When Marco Polo returned from his journey through China and India, he described having seen plenty of unicorns, though he seemed disappointed in them: "They are ugly brutes to look at, and not at all as we describe them. They have the hair of the buffalo and feet like elephants." He probably saw the rhinoceros, which was often confused with the unicorn.

There is a different version of the unicorn story from China. By tradition it is an almost fairy-creature that appears only to kings – to warn them of some great event about to happen. It is said to be gentle and quite harmless and to have a voice like the sound of monastery bells. When the great Genghis Khan was leading his army of warriors on a raid through the

mountain passes of the Hindu-Kush, they caught sight of a unicorn. Slowly it bowed its head three times – which so frightened these fierce fighting men from Mongolia that they turned and marched away. The Caliph of Mecca was said to keep a pair of unicorns in his palace gardens — a gift from the King of Ethiopia. But the holy city of Mecca was forbidden to Europeans and no one had ever seen them. The King of Ethiopia was said to be an expert on unicorns, and to have written a long letter giving a detailed account of just how to go about capturing one to the Bishop of Rome.

For centuries people searched across continents for this mysterious animal. The horn of a unicorn, the alicorn, was supposed to have magic powers. The very smallest piece of alicorn dipped in water was said to guard you absolutely against poison and inummerable other ailments too. In the sixteenth century, no king or prince worth his salt was without at least a piece of true unicorn's horn among the treasures of his house. There was a test to discover whether an alicorn was genuine or not: "Place the horn in a vessel and with it three or four live and large scorpions, keeping it covered. If you find four hours later the scorpions are dead, or almost lifeless, the alicorn is a good one, and there is not enough money in the world to pay for it."

It was worth much more than three times its own weight in gold. And the extraordinary thing was that everyone had an alicorn. There were some in Paris, Rome, Venice, Constantinople, and among the English crown jewels at Windsor there was a silver-tipped unicorn's horn seven feet long. In 1598 a German traveller to Queen Elizabeth's court valued the great horn of Windsor at £100,000 – the modern equivalent would be over £1,000,000. Right up until the eighteenth century the Royal Society of Physicians included unicorn horns as part of the essential list of drugs for any chemist on their register. There is still one to be seen in the Wellcome Museum of Medical History in London. But where did these elaborately spiralled unicorns' horns come from – certainly not from a unicorn!

The history of the Windsor horn is known, it was found washed up on the shores of Frobisher's Bay in Canada and presented to the Crown. A right royal gift, no doubt from the King of the Sea to the Queen of England! And that is precisely where it did come from, because these priceless alicorns came from a whale. Alicorns were the single tusks of the narwhal – not an uncommon whale. Now they are worth about £60 in curiosity value. As medical science and the knowledge of natural history increased, the virtues of the alicorn were abandoned – but people's interest in the legend of the unicorn continued. Travellers from the New World reported having seen them there; a single horned goat is still part of Red Indian legends.

The single tusked whale – the narwhal

Right up until the nineteenth century, French explorers in Africa reported seeing unicorns and made drawings of them. And over and over again travellers from Tibet produced more stories of unicorns from that mysterious country.

Until a few years ago, a statue of a single horned gazelle decorated the roof of the royal palace of the Dalai Lama. Perhaps that was what had been seen. It took centuries before it was reluctantly agreed that the story of the unicorn was mere legend.

Then, in 1933 an American biologist called Dr Franklin Dove carried out a simple experiment. He took a young bull calf and grafted one of its horn buds on to the front of its head – a simple operation. The graft took, and the calf grew up to be a one-horned bull. But that was not all that happened. This bull grew very big, strong and fierce, and the rest of the herd treated it as a king. Having one horn instead of two seemed to mark it out almost automatically as a lead animal.

Perhaps in the past, tribes in different areas in Ethiopia, North America and Tibet knew the secret of this simple operation and were able to plan and choose their own king animals for their herds. A useful and practical piece of animal management for nomadic tribes whose herds were essential to their way of life, but because it was a technique unknown to Europeans they thought it must be some sort of magic and named these creatures unicorns.

That could be the origin of the unicorn stories. Certainly part of the old unicorn legend is that he is a leader of other animals. The story is that, when all the creatures of the forest come to the spring to drink, they wait until the king, the unicorn, has dipped his horn into the water to purify it, before the rest of them dare to quench their thirst. His single horn seems to set him apart as a leader, almost like magic.

MAN OR BEAST

 N MANY of the mountains there is a tribe of men who have the heads of dogs, and clothe themselves with the skins of wild beasts. Instead of speaking, they bark and live by hunting birds which they tear with their long claws.

Partly-human monsters have always been fascinating. Mermaids were a mixture of lovely lady and large fish. The god Pan was half-man, half-goat. The Greek centaurs were half-man, half-horse. To a certain extent we still enjoy mixing animals and humans. Yogi Bear, Tom and Jerry, and Donald Duck are all more human than animal.

But three hundred years ago, strange half-human creatures were considered quite seriously to exist. The lamia was a wild night creature of the forests with a woman's face and a scaly body. The mantichora was a lion with a man's head and three rows of teeth like sharks' teeth. The satyr was a most rare and seldom seen beast. Then there were the dog-faced man and the cat-faced woman and many, many more. People with huge feet that turned backwards, people with tails, with

A lamia as drawn by a sixteenth-century naturalist

webbed feet, giants with one eye, people with faces in their chests and no heads. There seems no limit to our monstrous imaginations!

What is interesting is how ancient and how wide-spread these strange ideas are. The stories about wild men from the East with huge ears like elephants came from the ancient Greeks. The same creature appears in the story of Sinbad, though now he is grown into a terrible giant as well. Even more strangely there is a Chinese version of "big ears" described in a very ancient book which was written at about the same time as the Greek stories. There is also an odd Chinese creature without a head, but with a face in its chest.

There are lots of ancient stories about "little people". In a book of wonders *The Mirrore of the Worlde* written in the middle ages there is a chapter called: *Of the Strange People of Ind*. "In every region there be many peoples. There be a manner of people without wit, as madmen, which the King Alexander named Goths and Magoths. Also there dwelleth people that be horned; and people that are but two cubits high. This people is called Pygmans and be as little as dwarfs".

The ancient Chinese had similar stories about pygmans and so did the Greeks, who said these little people came from the mountains of Ind, or India. Although we know now that pygmy people really do exist, there is no existing race of pygmies in India. But perhaps once there were. In the Colombo anthropological museum in Sri-Lanka among the primitive stone tools collected from the past are some very, very, tiny stone axes. Were they used, once upon a time, by a lost race of little people?

It was less than a hundred years ago when the shy and gentle pygmy people of Central Africa were discovered. Then groups of them were taken away from their forest homes and brought to Europe, dressed in children's clothes, and stared at almost as if they were indeed creatures from some other world. They quickly proved how intelligent they were when one of them learnt, within a month or two of being in Europe, to play the piano. Some thousands of pygmies still live in the forests of the Upper Congo – but as they are introduced to the ways of civilisation and given clothes and houses to live in, they tend to catch Western diseases and die. Sadly, in another thousand years they may no longer exist, and this ancient race of people will then become a legend, with all the mixed up facts and fantasies that are part of most legends. Only three hundred years ago the large monkeys called baboons were thought to be at least partly human, and this is how they were described: "Their heads are like dogs and their other parts like man's. But it is the error of vulgar people to think that they are men. The west regions of Ethiopia have a great store of these Baboons. Some are beasts without a head, but with eyes and mouth in their breasts ... They know how to take kernels out of nuts, like men do – and find the meat therein. They also drink wine and eat venison which they roast in the sun. They are much given to fishing. They cannot speak, and yet they can understand the Indian language. Some there are, able to read and write, which is why the old Egyptians brought them into their temples and dedicated them to the God of learning".

The Egyptians used many creatures as religious symbols, and baboons – like most monkeys – show a kind of intelligence which is more like human intelligence than that of most other animals.

But the dog-faced man of legend probably came from another place – Madagascar, where there are monkey-like creatures called lemurs. The biggest of them, the giant lemur, has a head very much like a dog and a

"Indris! Look at that!"

body which is extraordinarily human in shape. It is called the indris, and that name itself has a strange history. The first European to see it heard his native guides call out "indris! indris!" He thought that must be its native name, but what they were really saying was "Look at that! Look at that!" But the name has stuck.

The indris lives only in one particular part of the forest which is daily shrinking as the trees are cut down.

Long before you can get close to the animal you can hear its strange cries, which sound like children crying. The creature itself is rather beautiful and very shy. Because none has ever survived in captivity for more than a few days, very little is known about the indris or why it should only be able to live in this one small patch of forest. But unless we do learn more about them and their unique habitat, the indris may only too soon disappear altogether and no one will be able to say: "Indris! Look at that!"

Some of the stories of fairy-tale monsters and giants of long ago have explanations that are quite ordinary.

When Ulysses landed on the island of Sicily he did battle with the Cyclops, a race of one-eyed giants, who hid among the caves at the base of Mount Etna. Other stories of giants who lived in caves appear over and over again, particularly in Italy and Sicily. Later their bones were discovered and put on public display – even the huge skull of a so-called genuine dragon was discovered and is still to be seen in the market place at Klagenfurt in Austria. Now we know that what they had really found were the bones of extinct animals, cave-bears, mammoths, rhinoceros and prehistoric elephants. A mammoth or elephant skull, from the front, does look a bit like a giant human skull with a single eye socket – especially without its tusks. The socket is in fact the elephant's nasal cavity, but if you had never seen a real live elephant, it would be quite easy to invent for yourself a giant one-eyed person from its bones – Ulysses' Cyclops perhaps?

Another strange belief of past ages was that somewhere in the mysterious East was a race of people with huge feet: "They have but one foot of which the sole is so right longe and so broad that they cover them in the shadow therewith, when the sun cometh over direct on them." A very quaint idea, or is it? The legend

This drawing of a "Big-Foot" is from an early travel book

of a large monster called Big-Foot still exists in North America. In America Big-Foot is big business. You can buy Big-Foot tee-shirts and ash-trays and cufflinks, and all the other tourist mementoes in the town of Willow Creek in California. The American Big-Foot is meant to be a giant hairy man who lives in the pine forests of the Rocky Mountains and has feet sixteen inches long. The Red Indians have many legends about giants. One is about a giant who fell to his death into a pit, and when he was dug up, was found to have turned into stone. A legend which is so similar to the European explanations of "stone bones" and "giant bones" that one can only presume the original story-teller had dug up dinosaur-bones and explained them as best he could.

The hairy Big-Foot legends, however, are much more recent. They began in Canada in 1811, with reports of an "abode of apes" in the Rocky Mountains. In 1924 a group of miners just over the border in the US reported that their camp was attacked in the middle of the night by hordes of apes. The place is still called Ape Canyon. The same year another miner described having seen a family of four of these ape-like creatures. He described them as being seven or eight feet tall, walking upright like humans, and having extremely large feet. At the time, he didn't tell anyone about them, fearing, he says, that no one would believe him. It was another thirty years before his story came out – and by that time reports of people in many parts of the Rocky Mountains finding trails of unknown animals with huge feet had become fairly common and the hunt for Big-Foot was on in earnest. But only one person has ever seriously claimed to have seen the creature in recent years.

In 1967 Roger Patterson and a companion were camping in a remote area of Northern California in search of the Big-Foot. They had been in the area for ten days without finding any trace of the creature. Then, one day when Patterson was about four miles from his base, his horse shied and threw him. As Patterson scrambled up, he saw a massive creature only about a hundred feet away. It was about seven and a half feet tall, and started moving away, walking upright, but not quickly, for it turned round and looked at him. Each stride the creature took was nearly four feet, and its footprints were fourteen and a half inches long.

It is a very lonely, wild area where there are few roads and which few people visit, and significantly it is an area where there are many bears. Bears can walk on two feet and they leave large tracks not too unlike outsize human footprints. But what did Patterson see?

Perhaps someone played a hoax on him. It has happened often enough before.

Seven hundred years ago when Marco Polo visited the East he wrote: "Certain people make it their business to catch a species of monkey having a face resembling a man's. They shave off its hair, leaving it only where it grows naturally on humans, in such a way that they have exactly the appearance of little men. They sell these to trading people – who carry them to all parts of the world".

While Big-Foot was leaving his tracks in the Rocky Mountains, across the other side of the world in the Himalayas another "uncertain" animal left footprints which started excited newspaper stories about the Himalayan yeti – or Abominable Snowman. A photograph taken in 1951 by an experienced climber showed a large footprint in the snow. The footprint was twelve inches long, and showed the marks of toes and a heel. It started an international yeti hunt which still goes on. Eric Shipton was on his sixth expedition to the Himalayas, and was on a reconnaissance with Michael Ward and Sherpa Tensing when they came on a trail of footprints, which they followed for about a mile, taking photos. Each print was large, and the length of stride indicated a heavy animal walking on two feet. The photos were sent back to London and caused a great stir, so much so that Shipton himself was flown home to tell his story to the Royal Geographical Society. Then at once everyone remembered stories told by previous Himalayan explorers. Stories of unexplained footprints, of unknown animals glimpsed among the rhododendron bushes, of strange cries heard at night, of legends of a wild man of the snows told by the Buddhist monks whose monastaries guard the high passes. The mysterious snowman was said to be large and very hairy, and to walk upright like a man. It was fierce and wild, and its very name would terrify the Sherpas. It was supposed very unlucky to see a yeti!

Sherpa Tensing Norgay – who climbed Everest with Edmund Hillary – said that his father had seen one, sometimes walking on two feet, sometimes on four. In the Monastery of Pangboche there is the skin of a yeti which looks very like a bear-skin, and the scalp of another. Hairs taken from this scalp prove it to be a man-made cap put together from the skin of a rare mountain goat. One monk said: "The yeti is just a bogey-man. Tibetan mothers tell their children stories about it."

So for a few years the Abominable Snowman story died down. Then in 1970 Don Whillans – the Yorkshire climber who was leading an expedition to Annapurna – had a new story to tell.

The climbers were just about to make camp for the night when one of the Sherpas looked up and said: "Yeti coming!" Whillans whipped round just in time to see a big loping creature drop out of sight behind a ridge.

The next night he watched for some time, and was getting so cold he thought he would give up, when he saw something move in the shadow. Then the creature bounded right out into the moonlight. It was a large ape-like animal, it bounded along on all fours and then disappeared into shadow underneath some crags. The next day he was able to take clear photographs of the trail of footprints it had left.

There are no large apes living in that area, only monkeys, and even monkeys are uncommon on cold mountains above the treeline. In 1870 a new animal was discovered, the Chinese snow-monkey which has been seen thirteen thousand feet up in the mountains of China. There could be more monkeys not yet discovered.

Yet the search for the Abominable Snowman still goes on, and at present a Japanese expedition is planning to spend two years looking for it, using helicopters.

I think there is an animal there – just that it has not yet been explained, and I'm sure it is not a hoax. But perhaps the Abominable Snowman lives in the dense rhododendron forests of the lower mountain slopes, and not among the snow-fields where it is usually hunted, and that is why no one has found it yet.

Recently I met a young American scientist who had just returned from the Himalayas, and he told me that one morning when he woke up, he found outside his tent a trail of large footprints. While he had been asleep some large animal had passed by – really close to his tent.

Coming on a set of unknown footprints can be scaring. When I was in the jungle in Borneo I was working with a famous zoologist, John McKinnon, who had been making a close study of orang-utans for some years. He had lived in the forest with them, moving, eating and sleeping when they did. He had become a forest man, quite at home by himself with his animal companions. Then one day, he was down by the edge of a river when he came on an unexpected set of fresh and perfect footprints. He could not decide whether they were human or animal. But he had never seen anything like them and quite suddenly he was very, very frightened, more frightened than he had ever been before.

The unknown itself makes us frightened. Once we know about animals we usually realise that they are more scared of us than we are of them. When I was last in Borneo myself, there was a particular kind of monkey I wanted to see, the proboscis monkey.

I first started trying to observe and photograph this

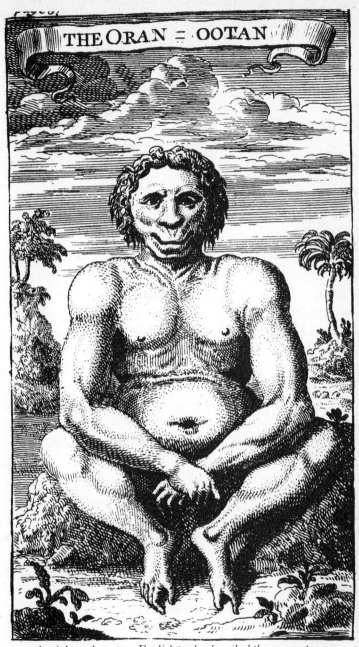

THE ORAN = OOTAN

An eighteenth-century English trader described the orang-utan as
"The Wild Man of the Woods"